In response to a resolution of the Legal Tender Club, of St. Louis, Mo.,

THE HON. JOHN MAGWIRE

delivered the following address in Turner's Hall, on Saturday evening, April 22, 1876:

I have been requested by members of the Legal Tender Club No. 1, of the City of St. Louis, to furnish such facts as I may think tend to show that the present high rate of taxation and rate that Congress has fixed for interest to be paid on the National Debt, is the primary cause that has produced the present conflict and antagonism between productive labor and unproductive capital.

And if it can be made manifest that the present high rate of the tax on productive industry has resulted in discord and strife, then the remedy, and the only remedy, is to lower the rate of taxation so as to produce a proper equilibrium; that is to say, there should be established some plan for an equitable distribution of the net productions of labor and capital.

Now, in order to establish and carry into effect a plan for lowering the present high rate of taxation (and when I use the word taxation, I include the rate of interest the government fixed on the public debt), for all interest paid for the loan or hire of money, is a tax on labor, and is paid by labor.

Now the question as to whether or not this high rate of taxation can be reduced to the rate of increase in the national wealth by natural production (which is at the rate of $3\frac{1}{3}$ per cent. per annum compounded), is a question of power, and it is with that question that I wish to deal.

And in dealing with the question of power, I have made no attempt at fine writing. I have confined myself to a statement of facts that are upon the record, and without any regard to the rules of rhetoric, the correctness of diction, or ornaments of style:

"When important interests are at stake, when momentous questions are to be considered, elaborate oratory is contemptible." —*Webster*.

By the law of nature, which, says Sir William Blackstone, is coeval with mankind, and dictated by God himself, every community has an inherent right to provide the means to relieve their necessities. This inherent right need not be declared, it is older than written constitutions or municipal laws.

An eminent Doctor of the Divine Law states: "God, when he created man, did not deliver him to the mercy of chance; He gave him the right of fulfilling his necessities, and has imposed on him the care of his own preservation as a duty."

And when the Almighty created the human race, ample provision was made for their sustenance: "Of the things pertaining to this earth, there are some which belong to us in common with all others, such as light, air, water and the soil."

Now, of those common gifts, no one is entitled to a surplus which will deprive another of a sufficiency.

There is, however, but one of the common gifts that man can be deprived of a sufficiency, and that is the one most essential for his existence, namely—a sufficiency of the soil as a right belonging to every individual. Without that sufficiency of the soil, man would be rendered incapable of fulfilling the duties imposed on him, namely—the care of his own preservation."

The main inquiry as to the amount of soil man is entitled to as a sufficiency, is readily answered in the abstract. It cannot be a less quantity than that necessary to provide himself with shelter, and he is not entitled as a gift to any greater quantity. Man, being provided with shelter, is at liberty to pursue whatever calling his genius, talents or tastes may lead him. But in the event of failure to support himself by his industry, or inability to find employment for a time, he is entitled to a shelter to fall back upon. And it is the chief duty as well as the prime interest of the State, to provide for the support of the individual citizen. The State never can survive the loss of the citizen, or the citizen the loss of his sufficiency.

I do not mean that the State ought to support the citizen. He must support himself.

But it is the duty as well as the interest of the State to provide that the citizen, with the co-operation of his means for labor, should have the uninterrupted privilege of taking to himself a sufficiency of the soil as a right belonging to him, as a common gift, in order that he may fulfill all the requirements of the care for his own preservation as a duty.

This, my friends, is a question that underlies the financial question, and one of far greater moment to the American people in its consequences, than all others that may arise in our system of political economy. This important question I have had much at heart for several years. I have hitherto elaborated it fully as to the plan for carrying it into practical effect, it has been submitted to some of the most eminent philosophers and jurists in the land, and by them endorsed.

I cannot argue the financial question without founding it upon the avowal that it is essential for communities to exercise their inherent right to provide the means to relieve their necessities whenever the exigencies happen.

It is upon this inherent right of self-preservation, one of the most sacred rights that God has given to man, that we derive the power to provide ourselves with all things needful for our preservation; nay, it is a duty imposed upon man by the Creator.

The necessities of a nation beget its attributes, and every community, being endowed with the power for self-preservation, can exercise that inherent power as they may think best for the common good.

"But there must be government and the obligations of obedience. There is no theory so clear, simple and solid."

The authority which commands obedience should be legitimately established.

Now, this brings us to the inquiry as to how legitimate authority may be established?

Wherever sovereignty resides in a nation: government belongs.

When John C. Calhoun was asked the question: "What is government?" He answered promptly: "It is the will of the governed." That may be true of a monarchy, but in a republic it is the will of the governor, that is to say, in republican America the government is the will of a majority of all the electoral people of all the States, hence, in our republic the government belongs to and is inherent in the people.

But agents to perform the duties thereof are necessary, and therefore are created—say a President, a Congress, a judiciary. This agency is not the government, however, nor is there a sentence or word in the Constitution of the United States which so denominates them.

In a monarchy the government and the people are distinct bodies—kings, lords and commons, as in Ecclesiastes, the clergy and the laity. In a republic the people and the government are one and the same; hence, the agencies of this republic, commonly called the government, are but a delegated body, and cannot, in the very essence of their creation, perform any of their functions without authority from their principal. When those agents go beyond their jurisdiction, and undertake to exercise powers not granted or specifically stated in the charter, their acts are void, and must necessarily be so, if the life of the republic is of any value.

Now, in order to settle the question of power, I have briefly referred to the facts of history—facts that I did not make, nor can I alter them. It is, therefore, upon those historical facts that we derive the power to provide ourselves with the means necessary for self-preservation.

The question now in hand is simply this: How is the present high rate of taxation to be reduced? The question of power to lower the rate is not open to controversy. This power resides in the sovereign and not in the agents, and can be exercised as the sovereign may think proper; that is to say, the agents whom the sovereign may appoint can be instructed by positive order to carry into effect the will of the sovereign.

The Congress can not, therefore, plant themselves on the power granted in the Constitution, to make money for any other purpose than to supply the National Treasury with a sufficient amount of legal tender tokens of sovereign power, which will enable that officer, at all times, to meet demands that may, from time to time, be proved up against the government, and that officer (the Secretary of the Treasury) is appointed for no other purpose than to keep safe the legal tender tokens of sovereign power placed in his hands, and to tender those tokens in payment of all proved claims that may be presented. This is all of the functions the Secretary is required to perform, and when he appears upon the floor of Congress, acting as a lobbyist for money rings, or making suggestions as to what uses may be made of the money token after it has left the treasury, he is forgetful of the dignity as well as the duties of his station, and he ought therefore be required to keep in his proper legitimate position.

Great stress is put upon the power granted to Congress in the Constitution in regard to furnishing the treasury with that which shall be a legal tender for all demands proved up against the government. And here again and again I repeat the fact that the Congress has no power in the Constitution, or out of it, to issue the token of sovereignty for any other purpose than is sufficient to supply the National Treasury with the amount needed to carry on the government and meet appropriations or demands against the government.

And the Secretary is prohibited by express words in the Constitution "from allowing any money to be withdrawn from the treasury, unless to meet appropriations made by law." It is so important that this prohibition be understood, and not misunderstood, that I quote the section referred to in the Constitution:

"Section 9, article 6. No money shall be drawn from the treasury but in consequence of appropriations made by law; and a regular statement and account of the receipts and expenditures of all public money shall be published from time to time."

Now that section of the Constitution leaves no such question as inflating or contracting the currency. It is a slang phrase, used by money rings, that has no meaning.

The Congress may place in the treasury as many blanks as they please; the Secretary can no more put the stamp or token of the sovereign upon them, or deliver them to a stranger who has no claim against the government, than the clerk of a court, State or federal, can issue an execution unless it is founded upon a judgment, regularly entered upon the record of the court.

Now we will turn to the section in the Constitution that grants to the Congress power to supply the treasury with blank warrants, executions or tokens of the sovereign power, sufficient to meet appropriations made by law, keeping in mind all the while the prominent fact that the Congress has no power, no authority, in the Constitution or out of it, to issue the warrant or token of the sovereign for any other purpose, or to regulate its value, except to make it a legal standard for payment and settling of disputes, than to regulate the value of horses, lumber or wheat.

The power granted is found in section 8, article 5: "To coin money, regulate the value thereof, and of foreign coin, and fix the standard of weights and measures."

To coin money? Coin it of what material the section does not specify. The expression is therefore indefinite and vague as to the material. If the words "to make money," had been used, that would not prohibit its being coined or made in any other mode.

Strict constructionists of the section 8, article 5, invoke the aid of the 10th section to give force to the words "coin money": Section 10, article 1. "No State shall coin money, emit bills of credit, make any thing but gold and silver a legal tender in payment of debts."

Now, no words can be more explicit than the prohibition that "no State shall emit bills of credit, or make anything but gold and silver a legal tender." Now, what does that express prohibition amount to? Every State in the Union, when it became necessary to provide the means to relieve their necessities, granted power to corporations, authorizing them to emit bills of credit, and the States were stockholders in banks that emitted bills of credit (and often very doubtful bills); and the people in every State in the Union use copper and nickel as a legal tender in the payment of debts.

In the face of these notorious facts it is contended that the indefinite words "to coin money," implies that it should be coined from gold, although the word gold does not appear.

We will now turn back to the Constitution itself, and inquire what were the powers granted in regard to making money.

The States possessed the absolute right to make money, and each of the States exercised that right, and made money of various materials, by fixing the token thereto by law before they made the Constitution.

The general government, in the Constitution, obtained full power to make money, previously owned by the individual States, and can therefore, by force of the grant if nothing else, coin money out of any material it chooses, or make it by another method.

But the grant gave no power to Congress that authorized that body to make money for any other purpose, as said before, than to supply the National Treasury with the amount needed to meet appropriations, and Congress is especially restricted in the amount needed.

To supply the treasury with a sufficient amount of legal tender blanks, in order that, when demands are proved up against the government, the secretary or proper officer may affix the seal, the stamp, or token of the sovereign upon it and tender the same to the claimant, is a part of the machinery of the government—State and federal.

The State legislatures furnish the local courts with blank warrants and executions. When the courts enter a judgment, the party in whose favor the judgment is recorded, is entitled to and receives a warrant or execution, with the seal of the sovereign State upon it, and by authority of that seal, he can command the proper officer to seize the property of the defendant in the execution, and have the possession of the same transferred to the plaintiff in the execution, or to some one who will satisfy the demand, and to execute and deliver to the plaintiff a deed for the property. This practice is going on in thousands of cases every day all over the land, and the title of property is transferred by virtue of the seal of the sovereign State, upon paper without using the money token of the general government.

Now the practice of the general government must be in harmony with that of the States, from which the federal government derived its power.

When a demand has been proved up against the general government, it is in the nature of a judgment and the claimant is entitled to his execution, legal tender or token of the sovereign.

The judgment of a State Court and a demand against the general government, which has passed through the various auditing bureaus, becomes a judgment not essentially differing from the judgment of the State Court. The execution, legal tender or money token, issued by the Secretary of the Treasury on a judgment against the government, differs from the execution or warrant issued by the State authority, in this: the execution issued by authority of the State, is limited in jurisdiction and in duration—it has power to transfer the title of the property of the defendant in the execution, but none other. The execution or legal tender token issued by the Secretary of the Treasury, is unlimited in duration, and its jurisdiction is co-extensive with that of the sovereign whose impress or token it bears; moreover, the token of the supreme sovereign possesses power to extinguish the execution and judgment of the inferior authority and power to extinguish all demands and obligations for payment within the realm, that is to say, wherever there is a demand proved up or a contract agreed upon a judgment or taxes, a tender of the token issued by authority of a law of Congress will extinguish the demand, whether the claimant accepts it or not.

Now, the value that persons not parties to a judgment, contract or obligation for payment, may put upon the token, is a question that has nothing to do with the power of the token of sovereignty. The token of sovereign power, whilst it possesses power to transfer the title of commercial commodities, is not a commodity. It is not founded upon any commercial commodity, it is not redeemable in commodities, nor is it founded on the property and wealth of the nation, for the government does not own the property or wealth of the nation; nor can the government take the property of the individual citizen and exchange it for the token; nor is it founded on the honor, integrity and good faith of the nation. Honor, integrity and good faith are very pleasant phrases used in writing and speaking; but outside the statute book there is no such thing. This assertion is founded upon the fact that there does not exist any exterior visible tribunal that claims to possess power or authority to decide questions of honor, integrity and good faith; and of course no such tribunal is recognized. If public opinion is invoked, nothing thereby can be determined with certainty, because public opinion to-day may not be public opinion to-morrow.

Now, this brings us to the question: If the token of sovereign power is not a commodity, is not founded on a commodity, is not redeemable in a commodity, is not founded upon the property or wealth of the nation, nor the honor, integrity and good faith of the nation, then it is incumbent upon the party who makes those denials to show what the legal tender token of the sovereign issued by the Secretary of the Treasury is founded upon. It is founded upon a law that has been approved by the Congress and signed by the President—a law that declares the legal tender token of sovereign power that the secretary has tendered to the party whose claim against the government has been regularly approved; that a tender of the token shall be a valid fulfilment of all obligations for payment within the realm, whether the claimant accepts it or not.

The question as to what may be the value of the legal tender token to the parties accepting it after it leaves the treasury, is not of concern to the government nor to what use the party may choose to make of it. The government is only concerned in enforcing obedience to law of Congress in regard to the token of the sovereign, the same as in all other provision of the laws.

This brings us to the question, where does the power reside that can enforce the laws? In the States the power is in the executive officer of the State, who can call out the militia of the State if there is resistance offered. In like manner can the supreme executive officer, the President, who is commander-in-chief of the army and navy, use that power, if necessary, to enforce the law.

But it is contended that a law of Congress that will oblige a claimant to take a token of the sovereign impressed upon paper, that has no inherent value in itself, as a commercial commodity, is an unjust law. It is, says some, repudiation to offer for services or for values furnished the government, paper that is valueless as a commodity, that cannot be sold in foreign countries.

Such a statement is a perversion of the facts. The government does not fix the value of its token of power, its value is fixed by the party that has consented to accept it for services or values.

The Congress fixes the number and amount of the token that will be tendered to those who may consent to accept appointments to offices the government needs fulfilled, but the Congress does not possess power to compel men to accept an office. If they do accept, however, they accept on the terms offered, and they are the exclusive judges as to whether or not the compensation offered is adequate to the services to be rendered or for the values voluntarily given. The Congress has fixed the salary of the President at $200,000 for the term of four years, but Congress cannot force anyone to accept that offer unless he pleases. If he does accept, he fixes the value of that which he has agreed to take, and so of all other officers.

When Carl Schurz was roaming over the country for the past three or four years, in his long, windy speeches denouncing greenbacks as worthless rags, the people could not forget that he accepted greenbacks for his six years' services as Senator, and that he exerted all of his ability and cunning in trying to get back to the Senate, and take his pay in what he called worthless rags.

And so it is when the government is in need of supplies. Proposals are received for furnishing the same; the government does not fix the value, that is done by the parties who offer to furnish what is wanted. In no instance has the government the exclusive power to fix values, except when the soldier is conscripted, his pay is fixed at the same rate of him who has voluntarily enlisted. When the government takes private property for public use, the value thereof is determined by a jury.

Now I have stated, as well as my feeble ability will permit, the facts which I think show or tend to show, the theory upon which our republic is founded, and alluded to the modes and instrumentalities necessary, in order that every citizen may enjoy the right to fulfill all the duties required for his own preservation.

Because of something wrong in the machinery of our government, where there are wheels within wheels, some have got out of gear, and this has, to use a mechanic's phrase, produced backlashes that are wrecking the entire fabric. When a machine is constructed on correct philosophical principles, and becomes deranged and entangled, the fault is to be found in unskillful or unfaithful engineers having been employed. This rule is as applicable to the machinery of the government as to the mechanical arts.

That there is at the present time something radically wrong in the working machinery of our government, is evidenced by the fact, that in the midst of a superabundance of the productions of the earth, capable of affording every individual in the land a sufficient supply of all things needful for their sustenance, industrial pursuits, that tend every year to add to the nation's wealth, by the general development of our resources, are paralyzed; our railroads are, with few exceptions, bankrupt; our factories, in many localities, are at a stand; others have failed, consequent upon their profits first, then their capital being absorbed by a high rate of taxation; thereby turning out of employment thousands of laborers, skilled and unskilled, naked upon the world, deprived of the means for shelter, driven by necessity, in numerous instances, to beg, to starve, to steal, to violate the laws. Many, unable to endure their sad condition, destroy their lives as if to afford relief.

Our jails, penitentiaries and alms houses are crowded with those who had been American freemen, capable of fulfilling all the duties required for self-preservation; men of genius and talents equal to any in the land are incarcerated behind prison bars, because, by necessity for want of employment and the means to provide shelter, they became vicious and violate the law. So it is with the children in our metropolitan cities, for want of shelter consequent upon a want of employment, they are exposed to temptations and fall into vicious habits that rarely ever can be eradicated.

There is an other evil that afflicts society more than all others. In its consequences, when we critically trace it to its source, it is found in the unjust and unequal tax the government has imposed on the laborers of the country. I approach this branch of my argument cautiously, because of its tender delicacy. It is, nevertheless, a momentous question that ought not be overlooked—it is the social condition of American women in certain localities. It is a well-established doctrine—indeed, it is a dogma of the system of civilization inculcated and enforced by the legislator of Judea—that society must be founded on woman's dignity. That dignity cannot be maintained if woman is deprived of her rights—her rights as spouse, as wife, as mother, her civil rights. Now, this assertion is founded on the fact that there are in some of the States from seventy-five to one hundred thousand more women than men (*vide* census reports). Where are the men that ought to mate those women? It is a historical fact that there are as many male children born as females; consequently, where there exists so large a preponderance of females, the same number of males did at some time exist in the same locality. But consequent upon the high rate of taxation on labor, thereby absorbing the net productions of labor and capital, the capital has been withdrawn from industrial pursuits and concentrated in government bonds and in national banks chartered by the Congress without authority from the Constitution; consequently, the men have transported themselves to other localities to find employment, leaving the women, that it is man's duty to protect and provide for, lonely, helpless, deprived of the means necessary for the fulfillment of the duties required of them by the law of their creation. As a consequence of their sad condition, many of these must go mad. I leave this melancholy statement of facts—facts that has touched the hearts of the purest patriots among us—and proceed to give the facts that has produced the evils that exist.

It is a fact that the high rate of taxation the Congress has, by law, established and collects in the way of interest on the public debts has, as a consequence, resulted in inflicting on society the evils now complained of—evils that cannot be endured much longer. Now, wherefore, was this high rate of taxation established by laws of Congress? Was it necessary in order to carry on the machinery of the government? If it can be made appear that it was not necessary, then the question is narrowed down to the single point of inquiry, namely: Who are the parties that ought to be held responsible?

The legislative department of the government is solely in the hands of and conducted by the agents the people appoint to transact their business in the Congress of the nation. If it can be made to appear that they have acted in a manner, that either through mistake or otherwise, in conducting the affairs of the government, evil consequences has been the result, then the first inquiry is: Were those agents capable, were they qualified and possessed the necessary skill for carrying on the machinery of the government?

Second. Have they been faithful in attending to the duties of their station?

If it can be made appear that those agents do not possess the requisite knowledge and skill that will qualify them for the position to which they were appointed, then the responsibility rests mainly upon the examining committee or caucus that recommended their appointment. If, on the other hand, it is found that those agents have been unmindful of the dignity of the position they occupy as agents of the sovereign people, or if it can be made to appear that they have been neglectful or inattentive to the duties of their station, then, and in that case the responsibility rests solely upon those agents, whether they are qualified or not.

We will now consider that part of the machinery of the government which requires the Congress to furnish the National Treasury with a sufficient amount of legal tender tokens of the sovereign power to meet appropriations made by law, keeping in view the fact, however, that the Congress has no power or authority in the Constitution or out of it, to furnish the token of sovereignty for any other purpose whatsoever.

Now we come to the inquiry: How has Congress supplied the wants of the treasury? And we will confine the inquiry to the period in time dating from the commencement of the war in 1861. When the war began, in order to save the life of the government, armies and a navy had to be organized and equipped. The time had arrived "when the nation could beget its attributes."

We could equip, and did equip, the armies and navy with all the implements of warfare necessary for carrying on the war. The army must have soldiers and ammunition, guns and cannon balls, supplies for feeding the soldiers. These we produced in abundance, and of such quality and material as best calculated to answer the purpose. The soldiers needed something to send back to their families, in order that they could have a support while the husbands and fathers were engaged in saving the life of the government, and thereby protecting the lives and property of those who remained at home.

The treasury soon became empty. The Congress possessed the same power to supply the wants of the treasury as to supply the army with implements of warfare.

All State banks that had emitted bills of credit founded on a false basis, failed. There was no money left in the country but the legal tender tokens the government had impressed on gold and silver. Those metal tokens were speedily hid away, and most of it transported to other countries. The government tried the experiment of offering bonds for the loan of gold and silver. The bonds of the government before the war, commanded a premium of twenty-five cents on the dollar. After the war commenced, eighty cents on the dollar was the highest bid received, and only for a small amount. Then the exigency had happened when the nation was forced to exercise her sovereign attribute of inherent power for self-preservation. Congress authorized the Secretary of the Treasury to issue a sufficient amount of the token of sovereignty upon paper to pay the soldiers and for supplies. The law authorizing the issue of the greenbacks as passed by the Lower House of Congress, made them a legal tender for all demands. When it went to the Senate for concurrence, the gold rings from Wall street were there, and protested against the passage of a law that would make the token of sovereignty expressed on paper as valid a legal tender as if on metal. Those gold rings brought their money power to bear on the Senators, forced them to act against their convictions by virtually telling them what Queen Elizabeth said to the Bishop of London when he objected to some of her whims: "Proud prelate, I made you, and if you do not obey, by G—d I will unfrock you."

The bill was amended in the Senate so as to suit the gold rings; the greenbacks were to be a legal tender for everything except interest on the public debt and duties on imports. Now, if Congress could supply the treasury with a sufficient amount of legal tender tokens, greenbacks, to pay the officers, soldiers and all needful supplies for carrying on the war, wherefore create a public debt? Wherefore stop issuing greenbacks and issue bonds payable in greenbacks? If the necessary amount of greenbacks, say one billion, had been issued, it would have been ample to supply the treasury, and neither bonds nor a public debt would ever had existence. But it was manifest to the gold rings that such a policy would leave them no margin, and therefore it was, that they stopped the issuing of greenbacks before one-half the amount needed to supply the treasury had been made. Bonds were issued, payable in greenbacks, and a tax laid upon the labor of the country to pay the interest, with the proviso that the bonds were not to be taxed.

Now, we will give the results of that policy:

There were issued, from 1862 to 1868, bonds to the amount of 1,854,866,150 dollars, and 1,235,879,416 dollars was received for them. These figures, which I found upon the record in the Treasury Bureau in 1870, show a loss to the government of 618,986,734 dollars, and a gain to the bondholders of that amount. The record shows that the bonds were sold for an average of fifty-five cents on the dollar; that is to say, the purchaser of the bond received a credit upon the National ledger for fifty-five cents cash, and by profit and loss account, forty-five cents.

But inasmuch as the bonds were made payable in greenbacks at our own treasury, thus keeping the debt a home debt, the loss to the government was a gain to her individual citizens, and was not, therefore, a loss to the nation.

After the bonds were put on the market, the greenbacks that would purchase bonds were denounced by the gold rings as a legalized fraud, in order to purchase the greatest amount in greenbacks with the smallest amount of gold, then turn the greenbacks into a bond, bearing a semi-annual interest of six per cent. in gold. In 1864, 2800 dollars in greenbacks were purchased with 1000 dollars in gold, then converted into a six per cent. bond for 2800 dollars. The gold interest on the 2800 dollars, collected semi-annually to the present time, will amount to twice and a half times the amount of gold paid for the greenbacks that were converted into the 2800 dollar bond; and, to-day, the holder of the bond can get 3200 dollars in gold for his 2800 dollar bond—a sum three times, plus 200 dollars, greater than his first outlay—having received meanwhile 2500 dollars interest in gold.

Now, can any one belive that the holders of the 5–20 bonds desired to alter the contract they had entered into with the government, when they purchased bonds that have proved to be so good an investment for their money.

No, the scheme for altering that contract did not primarily originate with the holders of the 5–20 bonds. It was a plan laid by the money brokers of England to get control of the money power of the American republic, by using Ex-Secretary Hugh McCullough and Jay Cooke as conduits in making a connection between the money dealers in England and the gold rings of Wall street, who control the legislation of Congress in regard to the financial question.

Now, this operation must be founded on facts, or supported by circumstantial evidence, in order to be convincing.

In order to proceed logically, we must connect the circumstantial proof as it appears upon the records of history. England's jealousy of our growing political power is notorious, and that if opportunity ever offered that England and France could, by interference in our domestic affairs, break up our republic, they would avail themselves of the occasion, if it should so happen. When the rebellion commenced, in 1861, both England and France exhibited unmistakable evidence of their desire to aid those who had undertaken to break up the government and found a new government, as they proclaimed, with negro slavery as the corner stone. Such a policy would have enabled England to continue, by her masterly statesmanship, control of the commerce of the world.

But after Secretary Seward had directed our minister at London to notify the sovereigns of Europe and the world, that the people of America would settle their difficulties in their own way, and that interference on the part of foreign nations would not be permitted, neither England nor France, after that notice, made any open hostile demonstrations of interference. Nevertheless, it is notorious, that the armies engaged on the side of the rebellionists were fitted out and equipped by England and France, with everything except the officers and soldiers. And this was done with a view to cripple American commerce, in order that England would not have so formidable a competitor as America in the markets of the world.

In 1869, in a letter of the National Labor Union Organization, addressed to President Grant, before he delivered his inaugural, His Excellency's attention was called to the following, which was published a few days before in an English paper called the *Manchester Guardian:*

"In 1850, England paid eighty millions for raw cotton, put it through her factories, and brought it out worth two hundred and forty-two millions. In 1860 she doubled the value, made the excess of value attained three hundred millions more; that the cotton famine in 1864, consequent upon the cessation of the American supply, had cost her fifteen millions in poor relief. Mr. Robuck and Mr. Bazely, members of Parliament, and Jacob Bright, at a meeting of the Chamber of Commerce, said: 'Englishmen are gradually becoming alive to the fact that Americans are in a fair way to supplant them in all the most coveted markets of the world.'"

It was manifest from the utterances of those English statesmen, that unless they could secure control of the money power of America, they could not control the most coveted markets of the world.

Says England's historian, Lord Macaulay: "That a Jew should be privy counselor to a christian king, would be an eternal disgrace to the nation. But the Jew may govern the money market, and the money market governs the world. The minister may be in doubt as to his schemes of finance till he has been closeted with the Jew. A congress of sovereigns may be forced to summon the Jew to their assistance. The scroll of the Jew on the back of a piece of paper, may be worth more than the royal word of three kings, or the national faith of three American republics."

The money power, Macaulay truly said, rules the world, and the nation that abdicates her money power or transfers it to a foreign nation, or to individuals who control monarchial governments by the money power, will certainly control the nation that has abdicated that power.

Pardon me if I dwell more at length upon the question of sovereign power. Unless a nation possesses power to provide the means for relieving the necessities of its people, or, in other words, the means for self-preservation, and power to enforce her own laws to that end, the government cannot hang together.

That the American people, in their sovereign capacity, do possess all power necessary for self-preservation, and power to execute their laws, has been practically and visibly demonstrated to the whole world during the late war, the history of which will forever stand as a monument of sovereign power. Never since the time of Cæsar, Charlemagne, the first Napoleon, Wellington or Bismarck, has the world produced greater masters in military science than the American officers who conducted the late war on both sides. Never has the world produced better soldiers. Says an eminent historian: "Give the American soldiers a just cause, and they will prove to be the best in the world. With all the activity of the Frenchman, the reckless daring of the Irishman, the steadiness of the German, and the pluck of the Englishman combined, they are a power that all the nations of the world combined cannot overcome, with their inexhaustible resources for support.

When it became necessary to invoke the military power to save the government, the Constitution and the civil law was swept by the board for the time being. And the military power, during that war, was enforced in a manner never exceeded in severity and seeming cruelty by any monarchial or autocratic government that has ever existed since the formation of governments founded on the theory of Christian civilization; neither has it been exceeded by the iron-hearted and steel-gloved hand of oriental pagan despotism. We witnessed, during the war, bodies of men marched out, who were prisoners of war, and shot down: men who were not guilty of crime themselves.

I allude to these melancholy facts of history, not for the purpose of finding fault or to wound the feeling of any one, but for the purpose of supporting my argument on the question of power.

It is, therefore, the military arm of the sovereign power that must be relied upon to enforce the laws.

When the King of England declares: This shall be a sovereign —that declaration, and nothing else, makes it a sovereign. When the sovereign people of the United States, through their Congress, has enacted a law that declares: This token of sovereign power shall be a legal tender throughout the realm—then it is a legal tender; and the facts I have stated show where the power resides to enforce the laws of Congress.

The legal token of sovereign power does not, therefore, rest upon any commercial commodity. The sovereign is not bound to exchange commodities for it. It does not rest on the property or wealth of the sovereign, or that of the individual citizen; neither owns property nor wealth that can be taken or made tangible by the owner of the token after it has left the treasury, to redeem that token or exchange it for property, unless the owner of the property chooses to make an exchange; nor is the token founded on the honor, integrity and good faith of the nation. These are figures of speech, as I have said before, that have no meaning, or at least no force outside the statute book.

Having disposed of the question of power, we will turn to the other question. The question now in hand is, how has the sovereign power been used, or abused, by the agents of the sovereign, in regard to supplying the treasury with a sufficient amount of the legal tender token of sovereignty to carry on the government, and to liquidate all demands against the government? not forgetting, however, that the treasurer is forbidden by the 9th sec. of the Constitution "from allowing any money to be withdrawn from the treasury unless to meet appropriations made by law."

Then comes the question: How can Congress supply the wants of the treasury?

If I am right on the question of power, I will answer the question of expediency so as to defy criticism.

After the war commenced, our statesmen, it would appear, for the first time, discovered that the necessities of a nation beget its attributes.

The law authorizing the issue of the greenbacks, made them a legal tender, and the bonds to be issued after the passage of that law, were, by operation of the law, payable in greenbacks. The government stopped issuing greenbacks and issued bonds—a fatal mistake. If a sufficient amount of paper tokens of the sovereign power had been ordered by Congress to supply the treasury, one thousand million of dollars would have been ample for that purpose, and not one dollar of a public debt would now exist.

The Congress had power and authority to supply the wants of the treasury with the token of sovereignty, and make it a legal tender, but Congress had no power or authority to supply that want with bonds or promises to pay, and levy a tax upon the people to pay interest on bonds not taxed. They had no authority under the Constitution for pursuing that policy.

Notwithstanding the loss to the government in the sale of bonds it was a gain to the purchaser, and the bonds being payable at our own treasury, in American money, keeping it a home debt, there could be no loss to the nation. The interest also payable at our treasury, the nation had the benefit of the labor necessary to pay the interest. But if the debt and interest be transferred to a foreign nation, the labor expended in paying the principal and interest would be for the benefit of that nation.

To let the bonds stand under the law and contract for which they were issued, kept the debt a home debt, within the jurisdiction and control of our government. And so long as that debt remained a home debt, the nation could control her own money power—a power, says Macaulay, that rules the world.

If the proposition was made by any foreign government, that we, as a nation, abdicate our political sovereignty and again become colonies, it would be considered beneath contempt. But when we transfer to a foreign nation the control of our money power, and become the debtor of a foreign nation, we put ourselves in a worse condition than to be colonies.

English statesmen were well satisfied, after the close of our war, that our government cannot be broken up, and that they have no power to interfere in our political affairs. But English statesmen and England's money brokers saw that if they could obtain control of America's money power, they could control American commerce and manufactories, and therefore a scheme was invented for getting control by England of our money power.

A clamor was first started against the greenbacks, that they were not money because not made of a commodity that could be sold in a foreign market as merchandise. A large amount of the bonds were purchased by English and German money dealers, who reside outside the jurisdiction of our government, but that is not of consequence as long as the bonds are payable at our treasury in greenbacks. The debt remains a home debt, no matter where the holder of the obligation may reside.

Those bonds were duly executed, signed, sealed and recorded, they were as binding on the obligees as on the obligors.

The Congress that executed those bonds acted as agent for both of the contracting parties.

The Congress had no power, however, to bind the sovereign, whose agents they were, in any such contract, and the sovereign has power to repudiate contracts that the agent is not authorized to make. That contract, although not binding on the sovereign, was for the time being acquiesced in, because the parties were within the jurisdiction and control of the sovereign.

But when the agents of the sovereign undertake to abrogate a contract that has been duly executed and recorded, and bind the sovereign to a new and different contract, their acts are utterly void. The Congress has power .to make treaties with foreign nations, but no power to bind the sovereign in contracts made with individuals in foreign countries and outside the jurisdiction of the sovereign.

Now, what has Congress done in regard to the 5–20 bonds payable, principal and interest, at our own treasury?

First, in order to have the way for changing payment of the bonds in greenbacks, to payment in gold coin, a bill was introduced by the chairman of the finance committee of the Senate, in March, 1869, and became a law on the 28th of that month, entitled a law to strengthen the public credit, as follows: "Be it enacted that all obligations of the government shall be paid in *coin** or its equivalent." The parties who planned that law did not venture to say gold coin, that would have been repugnant to, and repealed the act declaring the greenbacks to be a valid legal tender.

Coin or its equivalent? When two equivalents meet, there can be no remainder.

Notwithstanding we may logically demonstrate that the token of sovereign power is not a commodity, or an article of merchandize, the value of which depends upon the varying commercial value of any commodity; and notwithstanding that the progress in science has dispelled all ideas not founded upon correct philosophical principles; nevertheless, gold appears to have had a mysterious hold on the people of all countries from the beginning. The Hebrew historian records its existence in the second chapter of Genesis; and it would appear throughout the sacred record that by reason, perhaps of its great beauty to the eye, its immaculate purity and indestructibility, it was regarded as symbolic of, and connected with, the Deity. When Moses was absent receiving the law delivered to him on Mount Sinai, the people under his immediate charge, to whom God had manifested his power by repeated miracles, lost their faith and made a god of gold. When

---

*COIN—Wedge; stamp; corner wedge; die for striking money. The word is sometimes applied to wedging stone in masonry; a corner or jutting angle; a jutting point, as a wall; a wedge for lowering, raising, fastening or leveling up anything, as a cannon or printer's form. A piece of metal on which certain characters are stamped, making it legal current money; stones jutting from a wall; to make; to fabricate; to coin a word.

> Some tale, some newly text he daily coined
> To soothe his sister and delude her mind.—*Dryden.*

> This is the very coinage of your brain.—*Shakespeare.*

The word *coin* is indefinite, and may signify many things. Laws are made for arbitrary purposes; and words and phrases should be used that have a strictly classical legal meaning.

the Priesthood was given to Aaron, "a crown of gold was put upon his mitre, whereon was engraved Holiness, delightful to the eye for its beauty."—(Ecclesiasticus, chap. xlv., v. 14). And it is a fact of history, that pagan nations continue to the present time to make their gods of gold, and that there is a hankering after it among the Hebrew as well as Christian nations, although it can not be utilized by the latter for any other purpose than ornaments, and as an article of commerce that finds ready purchasers among the pagan nations for the purpose of making their gods.

Statesmen continue to assert, that gold was deposited in the earth by the Almighty, to be used as a standard of value, the measure of value, and the representative of value; and that the value of gold is determined by the amount of labor expended in producing it. This is logically true in regard to all other mineral deposits, such as iron, copper, lead, tin, zinc, coal, salt, and all else that can be utilized; but if applied to the production of gold, the logic will not hang together, as is shown by facts. Twenty laborers have searched months and years for gold, and did not produce an amount sufficient to support one man: on the other hand, we read of one man who, with no other tools than a common jack-knife, hooked out 200 dollars worth of gold daily for months; another obtained from one ton of quartz 42,000 dollars of value in gold, the cost of labor not exceeding that of quarrying a ton of limestone; three others, at Virginia City, have taken to themselves each 390,000 dollars per month of gold, being the net profits of their mines after deducting all expenses. If labor is to be taken as a standard of value (as it undoubtedly is), then gold can not be a fair measure of value. And it is no more a legal tender without the token of sovereignty upon it than cast steel, which never varies in price so much as gold.

When the Supreme Court of the United States, in 1873, decided that the greenbacks issued pursuant to the act of the 25th of February, 1862, were a valid legal tender, the act of March, 1869, was before the court; but no notice was taken of it. It had no meaning as viewed by the court; it is inoperative.

The court decided that greenbacks are not only the equivalent of *coin*, but the equivalent of gold coin.

The court could make no mistake as to the legality of the act of February 25, 1862; the intention of the statesmen who enacted that law, had been proclaimed at the time of its passage by Thaddeus Stevens and others, and again reiterated by Senators Morton and Sherman on the stump and in newspapers during the canvass in 1868, "That by the terms of the law and the contract, the 5–20 bonds are payable in greenbacks at our own treasury." They went so far as to denounce a party who would put any other construction upon the law or the contract, as an enemy of his country.

Thus the matter stood upon the statute book and the Supreme Court records. No profane hand was raised against the law or the contract until in January, 1870, the Chairman of the Finance Committee of the Senate introduced a bill that became a law in July of that year, which was meant and intended to have the effect of abrogating the contract that had been executed and duly recorded between the obligors and the obligees in the 5–20 bonds, and to repeal the law authorizing the issue of greenbacks in which the bonds were to be paid; not only so, but intended to transfer our national debt outside the jurisdiction and control of our government and place the control and management of our money power in the hands of aliens who have proved to be hostile to our form of government; thus abdicating our money power (a power, says Macaulay, that rules the world) by transferring its control to foreign nations—by changing our debt from a home debt to a foreign debt.

The bill proposing to change the law and contract upon which the 5–20 bonds are based, was introduced in the latter part of January, 1870, all of a sudden. Nobody ever heard of it outside the Senate until it appeared in the report of proceedings the morning after its introduction.

The title of the bill was as follows: "An act to authorize the funding and consolidation of the national debt, to extend banking facilities and establish specie payment."

The bill directed the Secretary of the Treasury and Comptroller of the Currency to prepare bonds, made payable by the government, to the amount of twelve hundred million of dollars, in Hamburg, Amsterdam, Frankford, London and other European cities, principal and interest, in the gold coin of those countries, which is eight to nine per cent. above our eagles. The plan proposed that syndicate commissioners be appointed, with clerks and experts, to travel over Europe with those bonds, expenses and commissions to be paid, sell the bonds for gold coin, bring it to this country, and pay off the 5–20 bonds in gold coin. The holders of the 5–20 bonds never prayed for the passage of such a law. It was a scheme invented by the money brokers of London and New York, to be engineered through the Congress by Jay Cooke and Hugh McCullough.

The real intent of the money dealers was to exchange the bonds payable in European cities in gold coin, for the 5–20 bonds payable at our treasury in greenbacks, thereby making our home debt a foreign debt.

When the bill was introduced in January, 1870, there was a committee of the National Labor Reform Organization in session at the city of Washington—a committee appointed by delegates that assembled in a National Convention, in the city of Philadelphia, in August, 1869. It was a National Convention, represented by delegates sent there to represent in that convention a majority of all the electoral people of all the States. The convention adjourned over to assemble again in the city of Cincinnati, August, 1870. A committee was appointed by the Philadelphia Convention to prepare a report upon the financial question, for the consideration of the Cincinnati Convention.

When the committee learned the full purport of the funding scheme proposed in the Senate, they transmitted to the Senate, and had published in the newspapers, a protest, of which the following is a copy:

PROCLAMATION No. 1.

SHERMAN'S FUNDING BILL.

WASHINGTON, D. C., Feb. 5th, 1870.

To the Working-men of the United States:

We, the undersigned, official representatives of the National Labor Union, composing upwards of four million of voters, and in connection with whom are involved the interests of twenty-five million of the American people, invoke your attention to a bill pending in Congress, entitled "An act to authorize the funding and consolidation of the National debt; to *extend banking facilities* and establish specie payment," introduced by Senator Sherman. This bill converts the currency loan made to the government at the rate of fifty-five cents on the dollar into a gold payment at the rate of $1.22 on the dollar. * * * It will appear, if that mode of payment is adopted, there must be collected from the producing classes, during the lifetime of the bonds, and handed over to the bondholders in interest, the aggregate sum of over $3,281,000,000, leaving the principal, $1,200,000,000, unpaid. This bill is skilfully drafted, and exhibits the outcropping of the craft. If the draftsman had $1,000,000 for his fee, it could not be more dexterously fitted for the nefarious purpose. It must have had its birth outside the walls of the Capitol, for the features of the money broker are stamped indelibly upon it. But, whoever is its author, we pronounce the bill, in the language currently used during the rebellion, a public enemy.

Signed by the Committee.

* * * *

The report of the committee appointed by a National Convention, was published in February, 1870, and unanimously adopted by the National Convention that assembled at Cincinnati in August, 1870. The report and the convention that adopted it, recommended that the law and contract under which the 5–20 bonds had been issued, should remain as it stood upon the statute book, and the bonds be paid in accordance with the law and contract, and inasmuch as the time had elapsed and that the government had the right to make a tender that the bonds be paid off, thereby relieving the labor of the country from a heavy tax to pay interest.

But notwithstanding the decided action of the convention, representing the people in their sovereign capacity and embodied in the protest of their committee upon the financial question of the nation, the Congress, the agents of the sovereign people, enacted the Sherman bill into a law that was approved 14th July, 1870.

When the act of July 14th was approved, an additional issue of six hundred million tokens of the sovereign power, put upon any substance by a law of Congress, would have enabled the Treasurer and Comptroller of the Currency to give notice to the holders of the 5–20 bonds that, upon a day to be fixed, the greenbacks would be ready and tendered at the paying counter of the bank parlor in the treasury building. Such notice of being prepared to make the tender, would from that day have put an end to the debt and interest, whether the holder of the obligation accepted it or not.

But the act of July 14th, 1870, requires that the tender be made in Frankford, Amsterdam, Hamburg, London and other European cities, not in greenbacks, not in the gold eagles of America, but in the gold coin of European cities, and no tender is binding upon the holder of the obligation for a portion of the bonds until after the lapse of forty years.

The holders of the 5–20 bonds did not ask Congress to change the original contract; they were content, as well they may be, to let it stand upon the record. Nor did the people, whose labor pays the bonds, pray for an alteration of the original contract.

The money rings argue that the Congress being the representatives of the sovereign people, are therefore the sovereign for the time being. This is true in so far as the representatives of the sovereign confine their action within the limits of the charter; but the charter was made by the people who are sovereign by virtue of an inherent right, and made for the guidance of the agents the people may appoint to transact their business. But the people were not made for that charter; they possess inherent sovereign rights and sovereign powers that are older than the charter, outside and independent of it—rights and powers that they may exercise whenever the exigencies happen that it is necessary to provide the means to relieve their necessities. Whenever the agents of the sovereign transcend their powers as specified in the charter, the sovereign possesses the right and the power to repudiate the acts of the agent and to declare them to be null and void.

In repudiating the alteration, or attempted alteration, of the contract to pay the 5–20 bonds, no injustice is done the bondholder—the original contract remains upon the record—he had the law before him upon the statute book when he purchased the bond, and if any alteration was made, he stands convicted of notice. If the alteration should turn out to be fraudulent, the bondholder looses nothing thereby; he having notice, must abide the consequences of the fraud.

It has been contended that Jay Cooke, in whose hands the 5–20's were placed to be sold (and he to receive a per centum of the proceeds), published notice that the bonds were payable in gold, the government ought to pay in gold. But Jay Cooke did not, in that notice, state all the truth—the government could pay in gold if it chose to do so, and had the gold. A tender of greenbacks, however, would be as valid a fulfillment of the obligation as a tender in gold.

In regard to the bonds issued pursuant to the act of 14th July, 1870, the agents of the sovereign had no power to bind their principal in contracts entered into with individuals residing outside the jurisdiction of the sovereign; nor have individuals not within the jurisdiction of the sovereign any power to enforce such contracts; neither the sovereign under whose jurisdiction the holder of the bond resides, or their tribunals of justice, can take cognizance of such contracts. On the other hand, if the parties holding the bonds bring themselves within the jurisdiction of the sovereign supposed to be bound, they are no better off. The government of the American nation has sovereign power but has no rights—it cannot be sued or brought into a court of justice. As to whether or not the bonds will be paid, is a political and not a judicial question. The sovereign may refer the bondholder to the original contract upon the record, and he may repudiate the alteration of that contract and assume the responsibility.

Now, I will briefly refer to the consequences that must result if that contract is carried into full effect, as provided for in the act of July, 1870.

Our home debt of 1,200,000 dollars, payable in greenbacks, is converted into a foreign debt which will amount to, when the last bonds shall become due, principal and interest, the sum of $4,480,000,000 (four thousand four hundred and eighty million of dollars). To this sum is added $10,000,000, appropriated to pay clerks and traveling expenses of syndicate commissioners.

A board of syndicate commissioners was appointed to travel over Europe under the pretense of selling the bonds issued under the act of July, 1870, for gold; transport the gold to America, and with it take up the 5–20 bonds. But that was not the real intention. The gold bonds were carried to Europe by the syndicate commissioners, there exchanged for all the 5–20 bonds that could be found, and for all that could be found at home were exchanged, and the gold bonds deposited for collection in Frankfort, London and other European cities.

Now, the amount of American labor that will be required to produce the gold and transport the same to foreign countries, sufficient to pay the debt and interest, is a matter that can be readily determined by simple rules of arithmetic. The facts of history show that the working life of laboring men, after they arrive at an adult age, averages twenty years, that the net production of the laboring man, after deducting food and shelter and allowing for sickness and casualties, is fifty dollars per year. From this data it will require the entire working lives of 4,490,-000 laboring men to produce a commodity to be transported to foreign countries, there manipulated into the various coins of those countries. If the labor is distributed amongst the multitude, the result will be the same, or in other words, that number of American freemen must be employed in feeding other people's children and impoverishing our own.

The scheme for increasing our public debt from $12,000,000 to $4,480,000,000, and transferring the control of our money power to foreign nations, was a masterly stroke of English statesmanship. But what is to be said of American statesmen who have allowed the government to become the debtor of a foreign nation in an amount impossible for them ever to pay.

That the fact of keeping our public debt outstanding, unpaid, and transferring its control to other nations has the effect of increasing the tax on all productive industries to an extent that absorbs more than the net profits, is evidenced by the bankruptcy of our railroads, the paralyzing of our manufactories, thereby depriving laborers of the means to provide shelter, increasing the temptations to vice, filling our almshouses, jails and penitentiaries with persons driven by necessity to crime, taxing the property and wealth of the citizen to support those whose necessities demand charity in a superabundant land.

The facts that I have extracted from the record, facts that cannot be gainsaid, abundantly show that the high rate of taxation has resulted in inflicting evils upon the productive industries of the country, that ought no longer to be endured, and I think the records to which I have referred, abundantly show that we as a sovereign nation possess power to apply the remedy necessary to eradicate those evils, that is to say, power to lower the rate of taxation to a rate that will not exceed the rate of increase in the national wealth by natural production.

This brings us to the question as to how the power can be applied so as to produce the results desired.

There are two modes in which that power may be applied. First, the natural and peaceable mode, the ballot; if that fails, then the bayonet. If it was a question that could only be settled by using the bayonet, then it would be one of short duration.

In bringing about the reform desired, we have no hostile foe to encounter. We can make no war upon the money dealer or the banks for deposits and discount; these both pursue a legitimate business under the laws. In neither the money lender nor the banks are vicious persons to be found. The capitalist loans money to his friend, never to an enemy; so do the banks, and they both act from patriotic motives. Next to receiving back the loan and interest, the lender is most pleased to know that he has benefitted a friend, or afforded facilities in advancing the general development and wealth of the State.

But the money power of the nation controls the ballot, the press and the legislature.

If the people whose labor produces all the property and wealth of the nation can control their legislature, then they are safe, and can afford to let the money dealers, the banks and the press take care of themselves. But there is no difficulty in controlling the press; that belongs to the people whose labor supports it, and must come to their aid when necessary to promote the common welfare.

The plan for controlling the legislature is simple, plain and feasible if carried into practical effect.

When candidates for the next Congress offer themselves to the caucus or nominating committee there should be a contract prepared for them to sign. They should be required to put themselves in black and white upon the record, stipulating and covenanting that if appointed by a vote of the majority to act as agents of the people in the next Congress, they will faithfully carry into effect the will of the majority in regard to supplying the wants of the treasury.

Those instructions can be embodied in one simple, plain proposition, namely: That they will pass a law, authorizing and directing the Secretary of the Treasury to prepare a sufficient amount of legal tender tokens of the sovereign power to pay off the entire outstanding public debt, in accordance with the original contract; and that public notice be given of the time that a tender can be made. This will stop interest and put an end to the debt, whether the holders of the government's obligation accept the tender or not.

I have referred to records which show, that the law of Congress, approved 18th March, 1869, entitled "An act to strengthen the public credit," is inoperative; and a law, such as here suggested, would render the act of July 14th, 1870, and the Specie Resumption Act, nugatory, and the bottom would fall out of all National banks.

By abrogating the act of Congress passed July 14th, 1870, so greatly increasing the debt, and making it a foreign debt, there can be no loss to the holder of the bonds exchanged for the 5–20 —no injustice is done to him. The original contract to pay in greenbacks stands upon the record. The alteration of that contract was a fraud upon the obligors in the contract to pay in greenbacks at our treasury, of which the holders of the bonds payable in gold stand convicted of notice. If the government refuse payment in gold to individuals in foreign countries, that will not prevent those individuals from presenting their claims for payment at our treasury, under the original contract.

Under the original contract, the amount of the 5–20 bonds stands to the credit of the original purchaser, or his legal representative, upon the National ledger; and on presentation of the bond for which the 5–20 was exchanged, must be taken as *prima facie* evidence that the holder is the legal representative in the original contract.

No charge of bad faith will lie against the parties whose labor is freely offered to pay the 5–20 bonds according to the contract. It is now a question solely for the people who assented to the original contract, and not for the bondholder, to decide for themselves whether or not they will submit to a fraud of which the holders of the altered bonds had notice.

The people that must pay the bonds, possess the right and the power to do in the premises as they please. They possess the power to prevent agents from being appointed to transact the business of the nation, unless they will give a pledge, in writing, binding themselves to take the initiatory steps for reducing the present high rate of taxation, by paying off the public debt in accordance with the original contract.

The people have a just right to demand such a written pledge, and have the power to refuse an appointment unless the obligation is signed.

The American republic is the first government, legitimately established, that successfully ignored the doctrine of the Divine Right of Kings. And we should be mindful of the farewell warning of Washington, namely—against the insidious wiles of foreign influence; (I conjure you to believe me, fellow-citizens,) the jealousy of a free people ought to be constantly awake.

Our government having been legitimately established, the law of nature, which gives us the right to provide for our necessities, and imposes upon us the care of our preservation as a duty, also includes the preservation of the government as a duty we owe to ourselves and to our children in our day, to our country and posterity.

TRADE AND COMMERCE.

I have purposely refrained, throughout the argument on the question of power in the Congress to supply the wants of the treasury, from mixing that question with collateral questions that may grow out of the multitudinous uses that the owner of the legal token may make of it after it has left the treasury and is in possession of him to whom it rightfully belongs.

As to the uses that may be made of the token after it has left the treasury, are questions that neither the Congress nor the Secretary of the Treasury have any right to meddle with.

Section 8, Article 3 of the Constitution, states: "Congress shall have power to regulate commerce with foreign nations, and among the several States, and with the Indian tribes."

This is a latent power that Congress is never called upon to exercise unless it becomes necessary to remove obstructions in the way of free transit in exchanging the productions of one territory for those of another. Foreign commerce is the same as domestic. The seas belong to everybody alike, and every nation alike has the right to protect their own flag.

But commerce, both foreign and domestic, is carried on by individuals in exchanging property and products based on actual values and not on legal or fictitious values.

For an illustration of this view the properties and values annually produced by the labor of the inhabitants in the Mississippi

Valley, including the Ohio, by labor skilled and unskilled, aided by machinery, is estimated in an amount equal to five hundred million of dollars; and it is reasonable to assume that in the multitudinous exchanges of commodities for commodities in the trade and commerce of the valley, not ten per cent., certainly not to exceed 20 per cent. of the amount in money is used.

The records of the clearing house in one of our metropolitan cities (St. Louis) show that checks to the amount of three and one-half to four millions of dollars pass through that bureau daily, and some days the amount has reached the sum of five millions. Now, not one of those checks were based upon gold coin, or called for gold coin, they were based upon the property and wealth of the maker that labor had produced. When a check is not responded to, the holder falls back on the drawer, and by operation of law, takes his property to the extent of satisfying the check. In addition to the amount of checks that pass through the clearing house, there is from one and one-half to two millions that pass daily through the various banks in the city, making an aggregate average of five millions daily. These checks are met with other checks, *ad infinitum,* and the final result is that the net production is absorbed by taxes.

BANKS.

Banks for the safe deposit of money are as necessary as storehouses and granaries for keeping the surplus provisions, or yards for storing lumber and other property.

The States, and not the Congress, have the right to grant charters to local banks.

When public notice is given that individuals or corporations have established a bank, for the purpose of taking money on deposit and for loaning money, the question as to the amount the bank may require the depositor to pay for keeping the money safe, ready on call, or the amount of interest the bank may pay for the use of the money, is one that concerns the depositor and the bank and nobody else.

The deposit is a loan made to the bank, the only security required is a credit of the amount to the depositor upon the records of the bank, and copied in a small hand book delivered to the depositor by the bank.

In like manner when one applies to a bank for a loan, the question of the rate of interest is one that only concerns the borrower and lender. But if the banks do not have an amount on hand to meet the demand for loans, as a matter of course, supply and demand regulate the price as in everything else.

If the bank has 2000 dollars to loan, and lets it to the borrower at four per cent., the net return will be the same as a loan of 800 dollars at ten per cent. But the results to the borrower may be very different. If the person carrying on business can have the use of 2000 dollars at four per cent,. he may pay the interest and continue to make a margin of profit; on the other hand, if he pays ten per cent. on 800 dollars, the interest will absorb all his profits, and finally his capital.

The amount of legal tenders in the treasury, and out of it, is a fraction less than fourteen dollars per capita of our population.

If the public debt is paid off, there will be outside of the treasury a per capita of thirty-five to thirty-eight dollars. This will increase the deposits in banks and enable them to lower their rate of interest, and thereby afford greater facilities to commerce and trade, and to progress in the general development of our resources—giving employment to all laborers, skilled and unskilled—and establishing a just standard of distribution of the net production of labor and capital, thereby removing all cause for strikes or antagonism between labor and capital.

There never again can be a monetary system established within our republic by State banks issuing bills of credit upon a specie, or supposed specie basis, as formerly, and as in England, where its bank, with fifteen million of gold coin in its vault, has issued sixty million in bills of credit. The bank sinks the interest on the fifteen million and receives interest on sixty million. So it was in our country when banks issued $300 to $700 in bills of credit based on $100 in specie, and often upon straws. The interest on the $100 was sunk and interest gathered in on $700—often at usurous rates. The people will never hereafter submit to a violation of the 10th section of the Constitution, which in express words, forbids the State to emit bills of credit.

As I have said in the outset, "The necessities of a nation beget its attributes"; and the way is now open and clear for the sovereign people of America to establish a monetary system to suit themselves, based upon the power to execute their own laws. As, when the King of England has declared, "This shall be a sovereign," that makes it a sovereign.

In like manner when the sovereign people of republican America has declared through their Congress, "This token of sovereign power shall be a legal tender," then it is a legal tender, and the power exists to enforce that law like all other laws.

I have endeavored to elaborate the question in hand, solely from a republican standpoint, without alluding to the monetary systems in monarchial governments. It is not necessary that our system should have any connection with those of monarchial Europe, because we are a self-supporting, independent nation, capable by the general development from year to year of our vast resources of supporting ourselves with all things needful, and therefore not obliged to carry on commerce with any European nation; whilst there is no nation on the continent of Europe capable of supporting their population and progressing unaided by the advantages they derive from commerce with other nations; and it now appears that the prediction of Mr. Bazely, Mr. Roebuck, members of the British Parliament in 1868, "that the day was not far distant when America would supplant England in the most coveted markets in the world," is being fulfilled. In 1873, our rolling mills received orders for rails from Liverpool, and we send our hardware and cutlery to London, and calico to Manchester.

It may be profitable, however, to refer to the masterly statesmanship that the quasi-republic of France has exhibited to the world in recuperating to her former station amongst the nations of the earth from the terrible helpless condition which she appeared to be in, at the close of the war with Germany.

I quote from the historian of to-day: "Never before had a great and powerful nation been so speedily and thoroughly mastered; rarely, if ever, had a brave and proud people been compelled to conclude hostilities with so disastrous results. This great nation, heretofore one of the most powerful and influential in Europe, seemed to be on the verge of political ruin. Such was France as she appeared before the world some years ago, and what is her condition to-day? * * * her financial condition is in most respects better than that of any nation in the world.

Her waste places have been restored; her industries have been stimulated into unprecedented activity; her exports largely exceed her imports, having made her a creditor nation. Gold has been steadily drawn to her * * * until the Bank of France holds in her strong room the enormous sum of three hundred millions of coin and bullion—(a sum three times greater than the amount of gold in the Bank of England and in the Treasury of the United States). France paid her indemnity debt of one billion of dollars to Germany in two years. It is true that the debt was paid with borrowed money, but it is also true that the French people were chiefly the lenders. The French debt, the largest in the world, more than twice as large as that of the United States, is literally a home debt.

Now the question arises, and is one of special interest to the people of the United States: By what means has France been able to retrieve her credit and recover from her misfortune; what is the secret of her recuperative power?

The historian comments as follows: The government of the United States changed the ownership of our national bonds from our own citizens to foreigners, by substituting gold interest for currency interest as to the 5–20's, and then created an absentee landlordism, which is crushing us as its counterpart crushed Ireland. France retained the national debt in their own hands; retained at home their own resources in men and money, to repair the wrongs of war and turn the balance of trade in their favor. France has thirty-four dollars per capita; we have thirteen dollars and fifty cents.

Statistics for 1875 show that France during the year imported 484,569,000 francs in value of manufactured goods, and imports of raw material amounted to 2,246,490,000 francs; food was imported to the amount of 779,884,000 francs. Total imports amounted to 3,672,266,000 francs; exports amounted to 4,022,162,000 francs.

The happy condition of France is solely attributed to her monetary system having been established on a correct basis. Her necessities, caused by the war, like those of the United States, obliged France to supply her treasury, and following the example of the United States, she issued tokens of her sovereign power on paper, differing from the latter, however, in this: The tokens of sovereign power issued by the government of France upon paper, is a legal tender alike with that impressed on gold throughout the realm, and therefore it is that her domestic commerce is carried on with her legal tender tokens stamped on paper, leaving the gold to be used in her foreign commerce; and her exports of manufactured goods largely exceeding her imports, the quantity of her gold is being continuously augmented until it now exceeds the amount in the Bank of England and the Treasury of the United States two-fold.

The legal tender tokens of the French nation, in the shape of notes of the Bank of France, will sell in any of our metropolitan cities, like the notes of the Bank of England, for a premium in gold equal to the rate of exchange between the countries. But the notes of the Bank of France are much stronger than the notes of the Bank of England—the former are based upon the sovereign power of the government and are a legal tender throughout the realm, whilst the latter are not a legal tender nor are they based upon the sovereignty of the nation, but upon gold supposed to be in the Bank of England, which is not there, nor has it ever been there in an amount equal to one-fifth of their bills of credit outstanding.

The legal tender token of sovereign power, issued by the American nation, is stronger than that of England and France combined; and if properly issued, would, like the notes of the Bank of France, pay a debt in any country that our merchants deal with.

www.ingramcontent.com/pod-product-compliance
Lightning Source LLC
LaVergne TN
LVHW011122110826
845150LV00008B/2225

9781418195113